What Did God Promise the Jews?

The Problem of Israel, Palestine, and the Church

Jeffrey J. Meyers

What Did God Promise the Jews?
Does Forever Mean Forever?
By Jeffrey J. Meyers

Copyright © 2026 Jeffrey J. Meyers
Athanasius Press
715 Cypress Street
West Monroe, Louisiana, 71291
www.athanasiuspress.org

Cover design and typesetting: Rachel Rosales

ISBN: 978-1-957726-26-7

Printed in the United States of America.

Quick Reference

Introduction

I don't have to tell the reader how dicey the subject of the modern nation of Israel is in twenty-first century America. Intense and sometimes vicious arguments about the political, social, and religious status of modern Jews have become a regular feature of internet blogs and social media screeds. American Evangelical pastors are passionately insisting that everyone, including our political leaders, must unconditionally support the modern state of Israel. This little booklet will be relevant to these contemporary concerns, without directly addressing every controversial issue. More than anything else, I'm interested in how Christians should understand what the Bible says about the Jews and their place in God's plans for human history. Once that is established, discussions about modern Jews and the nation of Israel can proceed without erroneous theological commitments about their divinely favored status among the nations.

To introduce the discussion, we can start with any of the promises made to Israel in the Hebrew Scriptures. Let's begin with the promised land. If God promised a certain land to the seed of Abraham, saying that it would be theirs *forever*, why do some Christians teach that the Jews permanently lost their right to the land? In Genesis 15:16, the Lord prophesied to Abram,

> ". . . for all the land that you see I will give to you and your seed forever."

That seems rather cut-and-dried. This promise is repeated multiple times in the Old Testament. Here are just a few examples:

> And Moses swore on that day, saying, "Surely the land on which your foot has trodden shall be an inheritance for you and your children forever, because you have wholly followed Yahweh my God" (Josh. 14:9).

Did you not, our God, drive out the inhabitants of this land before your people Israel, and give it forever to the descendants of Abraham your friend? (2 Chron. 20:7).

Your people shall all be righteous; they shall possess the land forever, the branch of my planting, the work of my hands, that I might be glorified (Isa. 60:21).

If Abraham's offspring should have that land *forever*, does that mean modern Jews have a rightful claim on the land of Palestine? Was it and will it *always* be their land? Is it really that simple? And what about all those other Old Testament *forever* promises and prophesies made to the Jews? Statements that appear to promise the Jews will always be God's special, favored people? How should we understand the Old Testament prophetic passages that seem to imply that the Israelites have a never-ending secure place in God's plan? Are modern Jews still God's chosen people? And does the oft-repeated promise/warning given to Abraham apply when we are considering how we are to relate to modern Jews and the contemporary nation of Israel?

> "I will bless those who bless you, and him who dishonors you I will curse. . ." (Gen. 12:3).

Just about everyone who reads the Bible will eventually ask questions like these. And if they don't arise from one's own reading of the Bible, one cannot avoid them for long in today's world. Not only do many in America's Evangelical Christian culture relentlessly preach and popularize their own answer to these questions but the unprecedented return of a people to the Holy Land after a 2000-year diaspora and the recurring conflicts in the Middle East cannot but cause people to wonder about the place of modern Israel and the Jews in God's plan for history. It seems like every time Israel is in the news American Christians can't resist proclaiming that it is a sign of the end times, and that Western Christians have a duty to support the modern Israelis because of their chosen status.

Are the Promises to Israel Spiritualized?

There are several ways to answer the question of Israel's place in God's plan for humanity. The simple answer is that when God said "forever" he meant it. There is no need to suggest that God set aside these promises. Nor should we "spiritualize" them and make them apply *directly* to the Christian Church. That is *not* to say that these Old Testament promises have no application to the Church. You'll see what I mean by denying the "direct" application of these promises to the Church as you read on. I do indeed believe that these promises and prophecies are fulfilled in the Church, but not by way of "spiritualizing" the promises, and not simply by the Church superseding or replacing the Jews. It's a bit more complicated than that.

Christian theologians have not always been careful about formulating the precise way in which the Church participates in these Old Testament promises to the Jews. In modern theology "supersessionism" or "replacement theology" are terms used to describe the theological position first expressed by early church Christians like Justin Martyr and Irenaeus that the church is the "true" or "spiritual" Israel. There's some truth to this, as we shall demonstrate. But there's more to it than a simplistic replacement of Israel by the Church. That's not the way the Bible presents it.

A recent essay characterized supersessionism as believing "that when most of Jewish Israel failed to embrace their Messiah in Jesus, God transferred the covenant to the Church, which then became the New Israel." Many Christians would explain it like this. But is this the best way of understanding the relationship between the Old Testament promises and the Church? Did God just switch out the recipients of the promises, replacing the Jews with the Church? This formulation is too one-dimensional, sidestepping the central element of God's eternal plan for both Israel and the

Church—the incarnation of the Son of God. As Christians, we know instinctively that Jesus is central, but we sometimes fail to make the connection so important to this subject: *every promise and prophecy given to Israel has a very literal, material fulfillment in Him.*

What I mean is this: The New Testament clearly teaches that the recipient of these promises (all of them) indeed belongs to a genealogical son of Abraham: Jesus. Jesus is literally and physically a bloodline son of Abraham and David, which is one of the reasons the Gospels present lengthy genealogies to establish this fact (Matt. 1:1-17; Luke 3:23-38). Since Jesus is "the son of Abraham" and "the son of David" he is the lawful recipient of the promises made to Abraham and David. In other words, all the promises made to the people of Israel are fulfilled in the incarnate Jewish man, Jesus.

Re-reading the New Testament through this lens will serve to make this very clear. Referring to Christ, Paul states "all the promises of God find their yes in him" (2 Cor. 1:19-20). He is the beneficiary of all the promises to Israel. Furthermore, as the resurrected, glorified, ascended, and reigning Jewish God-man, he lives forever. What that means, for example, is that Jesus, the faithful Israelite, now literally owns the promised land of Palestine. Since Jesus has inherited and rules the world, the land of Palestine is included in his kingdom (Col. 1:13-20; Eph. 1:20-23). The land of Palestine has been given to him (Heb. 1:2). He possesses it *forever*.

> And Abram said, "O Lord Yahweh, what will you give me, for I continue childless, and the heir of my house is Eliezer of Damascus?" And Abram said, "Behold, you have given me no offspring, and a member of my household will be my *heir*." And behold, the word of Yahweh came to him: "This man shall not be your heir; your very own son shall be your *heir*."

> . . . in these last days he has spoken to us by his Son, whom he appointed the *heir* of all things, through whom also he created the world (Heb.1:2).

This understanding then helps answer the charge made against some Reformation Christians of "spiritualizing" the promises made to Abraham and physical

Israel. Many Christians haven't answered the charge of "spiritualizing" very well. We have failed to emphasize the fact that Jesus was and is now a faithful Jew and, therefore, he the is both the True Israel and the inheritor of all the promises made to the sons of Abraham in the Old Testament. To confess the reality of Jesus' ownership of the promised land is not "spiritualizing" but recognizing a complete, literal, historical fulfillment of the promises made to Abraham.

Endless Genealogies?

Let's stop and plow this ground a bit more carefully. The answer to all questions about the promises made to the Jews is that the man, the Jew, Joshua Messiah, fulfills all those promises. He is physically a Jew and always will be. The genealogies end with him. He is the promised "seed" of Abraham. Paul, referencing Genesis, explicitly makes this claim:

> Now the promises were made to Abraham and to his seed. It does not say, "And to seeds," referring to many; but, referring to one, "And to your seed," who is Christ (Gal. 3:16).

There is no longer any religious significance to supposed genealogical links between post-AD 70 human communities and Abraham, Moses, or David. Regarding the promises made to Israel, Jesus was and is the only Jew who matters. And united to him, any person can be grafted into the olive tree of God's promises (Rom. 11:17-24). We partake of all the promises to the Jews in the Old Testament *in union with Jesus*. Israel was "the vine" planted by Yahweh, the vinedresser (Isa. 5; Jer. 2; Ezek. 17) but the New Testament revealed Jesus as the true vine and those united to him are the branches. Jesus explains, "I am the vine, and my Father is the vinedresser" (John 15:1). United to the ascended and reigning Christ, the faithful and immortal Israelite, we are graciously permitted to enjoy what has been fulfilled by and given to him.

> . . . so that *in Christ* Jesus the blessing of Abraham might come to the Gentiles, so that we might receive the promised Spirit through faith (Gal. 3:14).

> . . . for *in Christ* Jesus you are all sons of God, through faith (Gal. 3:26).

There is neither Jew nor Greek, there is neither slave nor free, there is neither male nor female, for you are all one *in Christ Jesus* (Gal. 3:28).

For *in Christ* Jesus neither circumcision nor uncircumcision counts for anything, but only faith working through love (Gal. 5:6).

That is why it is of faith, in order that the promise may rest on grace and be guaranteed to all his offspring—not only to the one of the Law but also to the one of the faith of Abraham, who is the father of us all, as it is written, "I have made you the father of many nations" (Rom. 4:16–17a).

Again, all the genealogies end with Jesus. The whole purpose of a bloodline "seed" is fulfilled in his birth, life, suffering, death, resurrection, and enthronement. The last two genealogies in Scripture are recorded in Matthew 1 and Luke 3. In those two final genealogies, Jesus is the "the son of David, the son of Abraham" (Matt. 1:1) and "the son of Adam, the son of God" (Luke 3:38). There are no more genealogies in the New Testament. They all end with Jesus.

Once it is shown that Jesus is the last Adam and the last Israelite, it's not difficult to acknowledge that the purpose of all the genealogies has been fulfilled. That's why Paul warns against "endless genealogies." That's why he counts his genealogical heritage as "rubbish" in Philippians 3:8 compared to his union with the resurrected Messiah. He warns Timothy and Titus about teachers in the church who continue to argue that genealogical connections have religious significance.

> As I urged you when I was going to Macedonia, remain at Ephesus that you may charge certain persons not to teach any different doctrine, to devote themselves to myths and endless genealogies, which promote speculations rather than the stewardship from God that is by faith (1 Tim. 1:4).

> But avoid foolish controversies, genealogies, dissensions, and quarrels about the law, for they are unprofitable and worthless (Titus 3:9).

In electing the Jews God had one grand purpose in mind—namely, to steward His Word and prepare the world for the coming of the Messiah. Once the Messiah came then Israel's genealogical purpose ended. Jesus is the final Israelite. He is Israel reduced to one. He is the promised "seed of the woman" (Gen. 3:15). He is the "seed of Abraham" (Gen. 12:7; Gal. 3:16). He is Israel's one faithful son (Gal. 4:4; Heb. 3:6). He is the elect Jewish Man (Luke 9:35). When he hangs on the cross and rises again to reign in heaven, he fulfills Israel's kingly and priestly mission in the world. Jesus has ascended to rule and he inherits all things, including the land promised to Abraham. And because of his accomplishments the whole world is renewed. As Paul says repeatedly in his letters, the only election that matters now is that which takes place "in Christ." God's election of Israel was indeed vindicated in the life, death, and resurrection of the chosen one—Jesus the Messiah.

The first-century Jews, however, misinterpreted the Scriptures. Even Jesus' disciples after his resurrection had to be instructed in the proper interpretation of their Bibles. They had been with Jesus and sat under his teaching for three years, but their skewed mindset had not yet been corrected.

> And he said to them, "O foolish ones, and slow of heart to believe all that the prophets have spoken! Was it not necessary that the Christ should suffer these things and enter into his glory?" And beginning with Moses and all the Prophets, he interpreted to them in all the Scriptures the things concerning himself (Luke 24:25-27).

> Then he said to them, "These are my words that I spoke to you while I was still with you, that everything written about me in the Law of Moses and the Prophets and the Psalms must be fulfilled." Then he opened their minds to understand the Scriptures … (Luke 24:44-45).

Jesus had to school his disciples because their minds had been poisoned by the way the Jewish leaders had perverted the law. The scribes, Pharisees, and leaders sidelined the proper understanding of the Torah with their oral law traditions. Throughout his teaching ministry, Jesus ferociously challenges the way the Jewish leaders had silenced God's Word by means of their extra-biblical, legalistic traditions. "You have a fine way of rejecting the commandment of God in order to establish your tradition" (Mark 7:9). These oral law traditions that Jesus despised became the foundation for Jewish life and culture once the Temple was destroyed and animal sacrifices ceased. Modern Jews are identified by their submission to the Talmud and Mishnah, which preserves not only the aberrant oral law tradition, but also completely eradicates the prophetic burden of the Old Testament as interpreted by Jesus and his apostles. Another way to say this is that modern Jews are not a remnant of Old Testament believers. Judaism is not the same religion anymore.

Location, Location, Location

Returning to the "promised land," we hear many Christians teaching the prophetic significance of the land of Israel today, including the coming centrality of Jerusalem and a re-built temple in the last days. But this is to ignore the priestly and kingly calling of Israel vis-à-vis the Gentile nations in the old world before Christ. The land of Canaan housed the special presence of God. It was home to the people of God. Canaan was centrally located in the ancient world to allow Israel to better serve the Gentiles in their capacity as a kingdom of priests to the nations.

Now, however, the promised royal priest Jesus has come—the one Israelite entirely faithful to his calling as a priest, king, and prophet. To have two priestly bodies or two royal entities would be redundant. Jesus now serves and rules from heaven. He alone is the new tabernacle/temple (John 1:14; 2:19-21), which is why the old temple in Jerusalem had to be destroyed. Jesus' land is the entire world, which he has inherited as the true "heir" and "firstborn son" (Col. 1:15-18; Heb. 1:2; Rom. 4:13). This is the real "scandal of particularity" for many today—that everything promised and typified in the Hebrew Scriptures is fulfilled in this *one* faithful Jew. The Israelite-centered old covenant is now obsolete.

> But as it is, Christ has obtained a ministry that is much more excellent than the old as the covenant he mediates is better, since it is enacted on better promises. For if that first covenant had been faultless, there would have been no occasion to look for a second... In speaking of a new covenant, he makes the first one obsolete. And what is becoming

obsolete and growing old is ready to vanish
away (Heb. 8:6, 7, 13).

The message of Hebrews to vacillating, first-century Christian Jews was that there's no going back to the old-world rituals and laws. The first century Jews needed to understand that they were living in a transitional time. The forty years between the ascension of Jesus and the destruction of the temple was a time of overlap between the old and new covenants. Nothing else need happen concerning the modern-day Jewish people or nation, unless, of course, our hope that they trust in Jesus and are saved. Once Jesus died and rose again, the last generation of Jews that were in covenant with God by means of the old covenant system was given an opportunity to repent and be incorporated into the Messiah's body. This is what the ministry of Peter and Paul "to the Jew first" is all about in the book of Acts. After that first-century second-chance offer, physical, cultural, and religious Judaism had no claim on or special place in God's purposes for the world. The resurrected, ascended Lord Jesus is the ever-living Jew in which all of God's promises are "yes and amen" (2 Cor 1:20).

The man Jesus is Israel reduced to one and "in him" all Christians are beneficiaries of the promises.

The modern nation of Israel or genealogical Jews have no special, favored status in God's eyes or in his future plans (apart from their trusting in Jesus Christ, of course). They are a nation and a people like any other. The land of Palestine is no longer a holy land, but simply a portion of the much larger inheritance given to Christ. The faithless, first-century Jews forfeited their title to the promised land. Jesus was given and now owns, not only the land of Palestine (which is most certainly *not* holy anymore), but all the earth. His Church united with him now is heir to the entire creation (Rom. 8:17).

> And if you belong to Christ, then you are Abraham's offspring, heirs according to promise (Gal. 3:29).

We should stop calling Palestine "the Holy Land." All such geographical and spatial defined holiness boundaries have been done away in Christ. Wherever a church is gathered, the place is "holy," for the Lord is there with his Spirit (John 4:23-24). Indeed, united to the true Israelite, Jesus, his body, the church is the new temple (1 Cor. 3:9; 1 Pet. 2:5), the new "chosen people," and the new "holy nation" (1 Pet. 2:9). The Old Testament "land promise" has been fulfilled—the ascended Jesus now owns the land of Palestine. But this is only a small portion of the world over which he presently reigns as Lord.

God's Favor

The Father has no special favor for any people, nation, race, or tribe that does not acknowledge the Person and work of his Son, Jesus Christ. "He who does not honor the Son does not honor the Father, who sent him" (John 5:23). Any prophesied future salvation of Israel would demand that the church have an incredibly awkward stance regarding the genealogical, cultural, and even national Israel. We would have to say that in some sense they are still "favored" or "special" or "chosen" and therefore be forced to "protect" their culture and people.

As we have seen in the history of the church's dealings with Jews, this leads to a love/hate relationship. How much better to confess that all nations, peoples, tribes, and tongues are equal, and treat them all accordingly? This need not lead to any animus against modern Jews. Rather, it simply levels the playing field. After Jesus and the change in the covenantal order and government of the world, the Jews are not central anymore. They are no longer priests to the nations. There's no one location where sacrifice is offered for the world. There is no temple. Jerusalem is not the center of the world. And the purpose of the genealogies has been fulfilled in Christ.

If the Father honors and requires us to honor those who reject his Son today, then there would be some special favor to be found with God the Father based on genealogy or race or culture apart from Christ—a notion that violates the explicit teaching of the New Testament. *Everything* in the New Testament screams *no* to this idea. As we have seen, there are no genealogies recorded in the New Testament after Christ's. This means that genealogies have no religious significance in the new world. As we have noted, Paul warns against "endless genealogies" (1 Tim. 1;4; Titus 3:9). Their purpose was fulfilled in the birth of Christ. How can the church treat some people different than others based on race or circumcision or the practice of Judaism's religious traditions? These all have *no religious significance* after Christ.

> For in Christ Jesus neither circumcision nor uncircumcision is of any avail, but faith working through love (Gal. 5:6)

Even the food laws of the Old Testament that set apart the Jews from the Gentiles are now defunct. Jesus "declared all foods clean" (Mark 7:19) and made Peter, a Jew, eat what was once forbidden meat before his visit to the Gentile God-fearer Cornelius the Centurian (Acts 10). If even an apostle was rebuked for continuing Jew/Gentile distinctions after the coming of Christ (Gal 2:11-14), why should Christians today continue to insist on such distinctions?

True, in redemptive history the Gospel goes to the Jew first after Pentecost (Rom. 1:16; Acts 13:5, 15, etc.). And after almost 40 years of having the privilege of hearing the Good News first, many of the first-century Jews repented and joined the church. But the Jews who would not repent and trust in Jesus the Messiah were rejected and judged. Paul turns to the Gentiles exclusively at the end of his ministry because God's patience had run out for the Jews (Acts 28:25-29; see especially 1 Thess. 2:14-16). In A.D. 70 Jesus came to destroy the old temple, and with its demise the centrality of the people and nation of Israel came to an end.

> For you, brethren, became imitators of the churches of God in Christ Jesus which are in Judea; for you suffered the same things from your own countrymen as they did from the Jews, who killed both the Lord Jesus and the prophets, and drove us out, and displease God and oppose all men by hindering us from speaking to the Gentiles that they may be saved—so as always to fill up the measure of their sins. But God's wrath has come upon them at last (1 Thess. 2:14-16).

The Interim Period & Childhood's End

If we don't keep in mind the flow of redemptive history, we will indeed get confused about Israel and the Gentiles. For, when Paul was writing, there was truly a basis for a *kind of* "love/hate relationship" between unbelieving Jews, whether ethnic or circumcised proselytes, and Christian Jews and Gentiles. In Paul's words, "As regards the gospel, they are enemies for your sake. But as regards election, they are beloved for the sake of their forefathers" (Rom. 11:28). This was the situation when the temple not only was still standing but was used by the apostles (Acts 3:1), even for offering sacrifices (Acts 21:23-26; cf. Num. 6:1-21).

Paul sometimes writes as if the end has already "come upon them at last," because that event is so close in time to him. Other times he writes more literally about the current ongoing transformation in which Jesus was creating, from Jew and Gentile "in himself one new man in place of the two" (Eph 2:15). Jesus, as the recipient of all the promises to Israel, now chooses all believing humanity as his one body (Eph. 3:6; 4:4). But while the temple stood, that process was incomplete, even though Christ had died, risen, and ascended. As the author of Hebrews states, "In speaking of a new covenant, he makes the first one obsolete. And what is becoming obsolete and growing old is ready to vanish away" (8:13). It is about to disappear but that hasn't happened yet. Then he elaborates, treating the High Priest's move in the tabernacle/temple from the Holy Place to the Holy of Holies as a transition between ages:

> These preparations having thus been made, the priests go regularly into the first section, performing their ritual duties, but into the second only the high priest goes, and he but once a year, and not without taking blood,

which he offers for himself and for the unintentional sins of the people. By this the Holy Spirit indicates that the way into the holy places is not yet opened as long as the first section is still standing (which is symbolic for the present age) (Heb. 9:6–9a).

So while the Temple was still standing, the old covenant remained even though the new covenant had arrived. The matter was not fully resolved until the old world of the temple in the Holy Land was abolished.

This transformation means more than just judgment on the sin of Israel. Jesus describes the judgment as going all the way back to avenging Cain's murder of Abel (Matt. 23:35). The reason for dividing humanity into Jew and Gentile goes back to before Abraham. God's original creation of the earth formed it into a pattern of sacred geography with a special Land (Eden, originally) in which there was a central Garden sanctuary (Gen. 2). That primeval arrangement demanded a split in the human race between those who live close enough to cultivate and guard the Garden (Gen. 2:15).

After the Garden was destroyed in the flood, God recreated the pattern by calling Abram and then giving his descendants the tabernacle and placing them in a new Eden, Israel. But the tabernacle and then the temple ultimately represented God's throne room in the Heavens. Jesus ascended to the actual throne of God, fulfilling the promises made to David and Israel. This was the upgrade of creation into a new reality and a new, unified, humanity.

Think about the implications of Paul's mission trips recorded in the book of Acts. When the apostle arrives in a city he goes to the local synagogue and reasons with the Jews, "showing by the Scriptures that the Messiah was Jesus" (Acts 18:28). Then something astonishing happens. The Jews who believed Paul's proclamation, were baptized, left the synagogue and were henceforth united to a new assembly of believers. They now no longer identified publicly as Jews but as Christians. They left their identity as Jews behind, having been united to Jesus and his Church. Those who were once identified as Jews and Gentiles now become "one new man" united to Messiah Jesus (Eph. 2:15).

Thus, claiming that ethnic Israel has separate identity from the rest of humanity is backwards. We are past that now that Christ, the true Israel, is enthroned. Indeed, describing non-Jews as "Gentiles" is also an old-world vocabulary. Gentiles don't exist anymore. There is no longer a split in humanity other than believers versus unbelievers.

A New Creation

In the new world, King Jesus, the true and faithful Israelite reigns from heaven. All Christians, united to Christ, receive all the promises made to the nation and people of Israel in the Old Testament (2 Cor. 1:20). There are no more Jews. There are no more Gentiles. This old distinction has disappeared. We live in a new world, a new creation (Gal. 6:14-15). There is only one Jew, and he is the inheritor of what was promised to Israel because he is the Greater Israel, the last true and faithful Israelite. Insofar as there are cultural and genealogical Jews that continue to perpetuate their religion after AD 70, is irrelevant to the Christian faith.

Christ has done away with the whole bi-polar division of humanity (Jew-Gentile) that was in force during the old covenant. This is repeated throughout the New Testament (1 Cor. 12:23; Gal. 3:28; Eph. 2:11-3:12; Phil. 3:2-11; Col. 3:11; etc.). The Israel/Gentile division served its purpose and is now obsolete. To try to resurrect it is to deny that Jesus is the true and final Israelite. As we have already noted numerous times, all the promises are "Yes and Amen" in Christ (2 Cor. 1:20). The Gospels indicate that he is the last faithful, bloodline, racial Israelite. He dies, rises again, and ascends into heaven to rule as Lord forever.

There is, therefore, no spiritualization involved in saying that the members of the new covenant Church, whatever their nationality or genealogical stock, now have access to all the promises of the Old Testament. United to the very human, fully Jewish Messiah who reigns in heaven, we, the church, are heirs of the promises in him. Modern Israel is no longer God's "son," but Jesus is God's Son and we in him are all "sons of God" and heirs of the promises (Rom. 8:17, 22-23; Col. 1:15-20). As the Apostle Paul says, "And if you are Christ's, then you are Abraham's offspring, heirs according to promise" (Gal. 3:29).

Importantly, not only are these things true today, they were always true, and the Jews at the time of Christ were repeatedly rebuked for misunderstanding their own Scriptures. Jesus himself repudiated the notion that being a physical descendant of Abraham gave one a special favor in God's eyes when he dressed down the Jews of his day for making such a claim (John 8:48-59). The Apostle Paul makes the same point about the status of the first-century Jews of his day:

> For no one is a Jew who is merely one outwardly, nor is circumcision outward and physical. But a Jew is one inwardly, and circumcision is a matter of the heart, by the Spirit, not by the letter (Rom. 2:28-29).

Speaking of circumcision, that ritual can no longer be the marker that sets apart the chosen people of God. The apostle Paul is quite adamant about that. In his letter to the Philippians, he mocks those who think that circumcision has some abiding religious value.

> Look out for the dogs, look out for the evil-doers, look out for those who mutilate the

flesh. For we are the real circumcision, who worship by the Spirit of God and glory in Christ Jesus and put no confidence in the flesh (Phil. 3:2-3).

Paul consistently insists that circumcision no longer has any significance in the new world ushered in by Jesus.

> For neither circumcision counts for anything nor uncircumcision but keeping the commandments of God (1 Cor. 7:19).

> For in Christ Jesus neither circumcision nor uncircumcision counts for anything, but only faith working through love (Gal. 5:6).

Circumcision not only marked out the people of Israel as God's chosen people; it also, being a bloody rite, was a ritual prophecy of the coming death and resurrection of the Messiah. Remember, the Lord had promised Abram and Sarai a child. But after waiting decades for the promised offspring, Abram attempted to sire the child promised to him by the Lord using his wife's servant girl Hagar. That story is told in

Genesis 16. The very next chapter narrates the imposition of circumcision on Abram and his family. In the aftermath of Abram's arrogant sin, the promise of a seed for Abram is reiterated, his name is changed to Abraham, and his flesh is cut off. Abraham attempted to fulfill God's promise by means of his flesh, his manhood. Now that flesh had to be cut off and rolled back so that a new flesh could emerge. From then on, every male baby would be circumcised on the eighth day. The eighth day is the first day of the new week, the promise of a new creation. Speaking of the resurrected Jesus, the apostle Paul explains this:

> In him also you were circumcised with a circumcision made without hands, by putting off the body of the flesh, by the circumcision of Christ, having been buried with him in baptism, in which you were also raised with him through faith in the powerful working of God, who raised him from the dead. And you, who were dead in your trespasses and the uncircumcision of your flesh, God made alive together with him, having forgiven us all our trespasses, by canceling the record

of debt that stood against us with its legal demands. This he set aside, nailing it to the cross. He disarmed the rulers and authorities and put them to open shame, by triumphing over them in him. Therefore, let no one pass judgment on you in questions of food and drink, or with regard to a festival or a new moon or a Sabbath. These are a shadow of the things to come, but the substance belongs to Christ (Col. 2:11-17).

The fulfilment of bloody circumcision was the death and resurrection of Jesus. The "circumcision made without hands" is not baptism, but the crucifixion of Jesus. The "circumcision of Christ" was his death and resurrection—the old mortal human flesh was rolled back, and a new glorified humanity arose on the eighth day. Baptism now unites us to Christ, when through faith we are made partakers of the benefits of his death and resurrection. What this means is that the old ritual of circumcision is now obsolete. Moreover, notice that Paul goes on to insist that not only is circumcision now obsolete, but the entire old-world ritual system has also passed away. It was always a shadow of things to come.

> Therefore, let no one pass judgment on your in questions of food and drink or with regard to a festival or a new moon or a Sabbath. These are a shadow of the things to come, but the reality belongs to the Christ (Col. 2:16-17).

Notice two things about Paul's declaration. First, everyone in the ancient world, both Jews and Gentiles, recognized that circumcision, food laws, and sabbaths were the most distinctive features of the Jewish identity. Even today, modern Jewish life continues these practices and others that separate them from the rest of humanity. Second, the problem for Judaism is that all these Old Testament practices were only temporary until the coming of the Christ. They were shadows pointing to Jesus. Jesus (literally in Col. 2:17, "the body of the Christ") is the fulfillment of the Jewish eschatological ritual system. The author of Hebrews says the same thing.

> For the Law has but a shadow of the good things to come instead of the true form of these realities (Heb. 10:1).

Earlier in Hebrews he designates the whole system of "worship" under the law as "symbolic for the present age" (9:9). The tabernacle, the priests, the sacrifices, the washings, the food and drink regulations—they were all provisional and prophetic of "the good things to come."

> According to this arrangement, gifts and sacrifices are offered that cannot perfect the conscience of the worshiper but deal only with food and drink and various washings, regulations for the body imposed until the time of reformation. But when Christ appeared as a high priest of the good things that have come . . . (Heb. 9:9-11).

Before the coming of Jesus' kingdom, the whole world was organized socially, politically, ritually in a way that is now obsolete. This organized cosmos situated the Jews at the center of a system that included a central sanctuary, blood sacrifices, purity laws, dietary requirements, and more—everything that the Law or Torah required. Paul calls this arrangement "the elements of the world" (*ta stoicheia tou kosmou*, Gal. 4:3, 9; Col. 2:8, 20). Before the coming of Jesus, the Jews were considered under-aged children, even though they were "heirs." Paul says that both Jews and Gentiles were "enslaved" to the "elements of the world."

> . . . when we [Jews] were children, we were enslaved to the elements of the world. But when the fulness of time had come, God sent forth his Son, born of a woman, born under the law, to redeem those who were under the law, so that we might receive the adoption as sons. (Gal. 4:3-5).

Paul says something similar to the Gentiles:

> Formerly, when you [Gentiles] did not know God, you were enslaved to those that by nature are not gods. But now that you have come to know God, or rather to be known by God, how can you turn back again to the

weak and worthless elements of the world, whose slaves you want to be once more. You observe days and months and seasons and years! I am afraid I may have labored over you in vain (Gal. 4:3-5).

Remember the problem in Galatia. Christian Gentiles were being seduced to keep the Law. The "days and months and seasons and years" in the passage above refer to the Jewish ordering of the calendar. For both Jews and Gentiles, to return to the old-world regulations would be to repudiate the new mature forms of kingdom living under Christ and to return to immature forms of servitude.

Blessing and Cursing

But what about the Abrahamic promised blessing? Is the Abrahamic covenant still in force today? Will those who bless Abraham be blessed and those who curse his offspring be cursed? Yes, but... we must take into account everything we've learned thus far. The Abrahamic covenant was renewed and transformed by the Mosaic covenant. Then the Mosaic covenant was renewed and transformed by the Davidic covenant. Later the Davidic covenant underwent changes after the exile and something new came from the old. There was a sequence of "new" covenants even in the Old Testament. Each time this happened the older covenant was taken up into the new one with significant changes. It's not simply that each covenant ended and a new one took its place. Each old covenant was transfigured into a new one.

Finally, all of this comes to completion in what we call the New Testament or New Covenant with the birth, life, death, resurrection, and ascension of Jesus. Every one of the older covenants is fulfilled in him and all of the promises from all these previous covenants are "yes" and "amen" only in him (2 Cor. 1:20). Jesus fulfills the Abrahamic covenant. He is a bloodline "son" of Abraham (Matt. 1), the "seed" promised to Abraham. Paul makes that clear in Galatians.

> Now the promises were made to Abraham and to his offspring. It does not say, "And to offsprings," referring to many, but referring to one, "And to your offspring," who is Christ (Gal. 3:16).

That's why the New Testament, especially Paul is so adamant about the fact that the people of God are those who by faith are united to Christ. All who bless Jesus are blessed. If you love and bless Jesus, the seed of Abraham, you are blessed. If you curse Jesus, you are cursed.

> If anyone has no love for the Lord, let him
> be accursed (1 Cor. 16:22).

That is the fulfillment of the Abrahamic covenant with respect to blessings and curses. The Abrahamic covenant has nothing to do with how the United States, or any other country treats the modern nation of Israel. To suggest that God loves or favors present-day Jews apart from their trusting in Christ is appalling and contrary to the explicit teaching of the New Testament, especially since today they are vocal enemies of the church and of the Gospel.

Further, the apostles taught that the Church is now called to fulfill what was once Israel's vocation.

> But you are a chosen race, a royal priesthood,
> a holy nation, a people for his own posses-
> sion, that you may proclaim the excellencies
> of him who called you out of darkness into
> his marvelous light (1 Pet. 2:9).

There are no unfulfilled promises that apply to anyone other than Jesus Christ and the Church in union with him. What Paul speaks of in Romans 11 is *future* to Paul, but past for us. It was fulfilled prior to God putting an end to the old world in A.D. 70 when the apostate Jews were judged and the temple was destroyed, as Jesus prophesied in Matthew 24, Mark 13, and Luke 21. This is not the place for a detailed exposition of Romans 11. Let me just say that everything promised in Romans 11 came to pass in the first century, as has been recorded in Acts and Revelation. The book of Acts records the "second chance" given to the Jews, when for forty years they heard the witness of the Apostles to Messiah Jesus and the offer of forgiveness. Luke records in Acts that the mission to the Jews was successful. All Isreal was saved. Revelation 7:1-8 records the conversion (and martyrdom?) of 144,000 Jews before the judgment on Jerusalem in the first century. They are distinguished from the multitude described in the second half of Revelation 7. These are from the "tribes of Israel." The 144,000 number is symbolic, the square of 12, Israel's number. This fulfills the promise of salvation for "the remnant" that Paul foresees in Romans 11. In the interim period before the fall of Jerusalem the olive tree was pruned of unbelieving Jews and believing Gentiles were grafted in.

At the *present time* there is a remnant chosen
by grace (Rom. 11:5).

. . . so they too [Jews] have *now* been dis-
obedient in order that by the mercy shown
to you [Gentiles] they also may *now* receive
mercy (Rom. 11:31).

Paul is talking about what was happening in the
first century, not something thousands or tens of thousands of years in the future. But what about Paul's
declaration that "the gifts and calling of God are irrevocable" (Rom. 1:29)? Don't misinterpret that state-
ment. In every previous age and successive covenant,
the chosen people were whittled down to a remnant
that were faithful to Israel's gifts and calling. So too,
in the first century, at the end of Israel's history, there
would be those who recognized their Messiah and
united with him by faith. And there would be others
who squandered their gifts and abandoned their calling only to be condemned by the Lord. When the full
number of first-century Jews were saved and the Lord
came in judgment on Jerusalem, the way was clear for
the world-wide mission of the Church to proceed. Is-

rael's irrevocable gifts and vocation would, from that time forward, be secure in the risen Jewish Messiah Jesus. He now is the faithful one, the final true remnant of Israel who lives and reigns forever, endowed with all the gifts promised to Israel and fulfilling their calling as Priest, King, and Prophet.

When Paul says that the "gifts and calling of God or irrevocable" (Rom. 11:29) this was not a contradiction of what was on the near horizon for the Jews—the destruction of the temple, the cessation of animal sacrifices, the cancelation of the Levites' priestly vocation, the end of sabbaths, etc.—in other words, the kingdom being taken from the Jews and given to Jesus and his Church. In a few pages I will list all the old-world "gifts" that have been finalized with the coming of Jesus' kingdom. The loss of these gifts, however, was no simple revocation, but the prophetic *completion* of Israel's gifts and calling by Jesus and his people. As the Lord himself prophesied:

> "Therefore I tell you, the kingdom of God
> will be taken away from you and given to a
> people producing its fruits" (Matt. 21:43).

Israel's vocation was to be priests to the nations, showing the Gentiles the grace and wisdom of the Lord. God holds out to them the promise of a fruitful ministry to the world if they remained true to their calling as a nation.

> Keep them and do them, for that will be your wisdom and your understanding in the sight of the peoples, who, when they hear all these statutes, will say, 'Surely this great nation is a wise and understanding people." (Deut. 4:6).

> I will make you as a light for the nations, that my salvation may reach to the end of the earth (Isa. 49:6).

The apostle Paul chides the first-century Jews for not fulfilling their divine calling.

> But if you call yourself a Jew and rely on the law and boast in God and know his will and approve what is excellent, because you are instructed from the law; and if you are sure

that you yourself are a guide to the blind, a light to those who are in darkness, an instructor of the foolish, a teacher of children, having in the law the embodiment of knowledge and truth— you then who teach others, do you not teach yourself? While you preach against stealing, do you steal? You who say that one must not commit adultery, do you commit adultery? You who abhor idols, do you rob temples? You who boast in the law dishonor God by breaking the law. For, as it is written, "The name of God is blasphemed among the Gentiles because of you" (Rom. 2:17-24).

This vocation/calling of being wisdom and light to the Gentiles is now being faithfully accomplished by the ever-living, ever-reigning Lord Jesus. Israel's calling has not be revoked. Rather, her calling has now come to it's proper end with the faithful service of the Jewish Priest and King, Jesus the Messiah. In Christ "are hidden all the treasures of wisdom and knowledge" (Col. 2:3). Jesus confirms his calling as "the light of the world" (John 8:12; 9:5). After taking up the baby Jesus in his arms Simeon sings,

> Lord, now you are letting your servant
>> depart in peace,
>>> according to your Word;
>> for my eyes have seen your salvation
>>> that you have prepared in the presence
>>>> of all peoples,
>> a light for revelation to the Gentiles,
>>> and for glory to your people Israel"
> (Luke 2:29-32).

Some have thought that the disciples' question at the beginning of the book of Acts means that there is still a future "kingdom" for Israel. "Lord, will you at this time restore the kingdom to Israel?" Jesus sidesteps the question and tells them it's not for them to know the "times and seasons that the Father has fixed" (Acts 1:6-7). At this point in the story the disciples are more than a little naïve. They don't realize that Israel has forfeited the right to the kingdom or that she will do so as the apostolic age progresses. They need to experience Israel's apostasy. And they will. Their question functions as a foil for the coming narrative of Israel's failure in the book of Acts. Although many Jews repent and join the apostolic church, the leaders of the nation do not. They become vicious persecutors of Jesus' church. Repeatedly they are shown to be the source of lawless violence in the empire. It's hard to overstate how wicked the Jews become in the story of Acts.

As the story unfolds, Acts describes the apostasy of the rest of the Jews even as the faithful remnant hear the Gospel and are culled out of the synagogues into the church:

> They crucified their Messiah, handing him over to lawless men (Acts 2:23)

> Their temple is impotent (Acts 3:1-10)

> They killed the Author of Life (Acts 3:15)

> They arrested apostles and are equated with the raging, plotting Gentiles (Acts 4)

> They sought to kill the apostles but settle for beating them (Acts 5)

They stoned Stephen (Acts 7), who warns them that they are stiff-necked, uncircumcised and always resist the Holy Spirit (Acts 7:51)

They began a great persecution against Christians in Jerusalem (Acts 8:1)

They dragged off men and women for prison (Acts 8:3)

The Jerusalem officials empowered agents like Saul to capture Christians and bring them back to Jerusalem for interrogation and execution (Acts 9:1-2; 26:10-11)

They plotted to kill the converted Saul (Acts 9:23)

They killed the apostle James and imprisoned Peter (Acts 12)

King Herod is so evil an angel of the Lord had to strike him down (Acts 12:23).

They functioned as false wise men leading the Romans astray (Acts 13:4-12; Rom. 2:24)

They repeatedly reviled and attacked the Apostle Paul (Acts 13:45)

They poisoned the minds of the Gentiles against Paul (Acts 14:2)

They pursued Paul from town to town and stoned him (Act 14:19; 2 Cor. 11)

They agitated and stirred up mobs of evil men to assault Paul (Acts 17:5,13)

They brought false charges against Paul before Roman magistrates (Acts 18:12)

They arrested Paul in Jerusalem and were going to kill him (Acts 21:30-31)

The chief priests and elders in Jerusalem plotted to assassinate Paul (Acts 23:12-15)

They brought false charges against Paul to the Roman governors, Felix and Festus (Acts 24-25)

They were acting out Isaiah the prophet's indictment and forfeited the benefit of Paul's ministry at the end of the book of Acts (Acts 28:23-29)

Is it any wonder that Paul characterizes the first-century Jews as those "who killed both the Lord Jesus and the prophets, and drove us out, and displease

God and oppose all mankind by hindering us from speaking to the Gentiles that they may be saved—so as always to fill up the measure of their sins. But God's wrath has come upon them at last" (1 Thess. 2:14-16). The apostles go to the Jews first, but in the end, Paul is done with them and focuses exclusively on the Gentiles (Acts 28:23-28). When the story is told of the 40 years of Israel's opportunity to repent, in the end Jerusalem becomes a new Egypt and Sodom, out of which the faithful must flee (Rev. 11:8). Jesus' Olivet prophecies have come to pass (Matt. 24, Mark 13, Luke 21). This is what Jesus predicted in Matthew 23:29-36:

> Woe to you, scribes and Pharisees, hypocrites! For you build the tombs of the prophets and decorate the monuments of the righteous, saying, 'If we had lived in the days of our fathers, we would not have taken part with them in shedding the blood of the prophets.' Thus you witness against yourselves that you are sons of those who murdered the prophets. Fill up, then, the measure of your fathers. You serpents, you brood of vipers, how are you to escape being sen-

tenced to hell? Therefore I send you prophets and wise men and scribes, some of whom you will kill and crucify, and some you will flog in your synagogues and persecute from town to town, so that on you may come all the righteous blood shed on earth, from the blood of innocent Abel to the blood of Zechariah the son of Barachiah, whom you murdered between the sanctuary and the altar. Truly, I say to you, all these things will come upon this generation.

Conclusion

The big takeaway is this: all the promises and prophecies made to the people of God in the Old Testament
apply *directly* to Jesus as heir, the last faithful Jew, and
then *indirectly* to the Church as co-heirs because she
is *united* to the resurrected, glorified, ascended Son of
David. Jesus and his Church—what has been called *to-
tus Christus*—are the new Israel.

The claim that there is still some special status or
favor for genealogical, cultural, religious, or national
Israel, even if it's just the promise of an unbroken racial bloodline, is horribly misguided. The purpose of
the genealogies of Israel is fulfilled in Christ. He is the
last genealogical Jew with prophetic significance. God
gave the last generation of Jews alive during that time

(AD 30-70) a chance to repent and be united to the true and faithful Israelite, the Greater Moses and David, who now reigns in heaven. But after that, the New Testament makes clear there is no ongoing significance in continuing a genealogical or cultural Judaism. The "forever" promises and prophecies were ultimately made and fulfilled for Jesus Christ and his Bride, the Church, who is now "one flesh" with him.

The old-world bifurcation of humanity into 1) a chosen, priestly nation (Israel), and 2) the other nations (Gentiles), has been dissolved. The distinction of Israel as a holy nation, a chosen people served its eschatological purpose: to prepare the world for the coming Messiah. Virtually everything about that archaic world relating to this partitioning of mankind is now obsolete with the advent of Jesus and his kingdom, including especially the bipolar division of humanity into Jews and Gentiles. After a time of transition (from the ascension of Jesus to the destruction of the temple forty years later), the old system was deconstructed. Consider the radical nature of the changes, and what has passed away:

1. No central sanctuary/temple (Matt. 24:2; Heb. 9:11-12)

2. No holy city/Jerusalem (John 4:21; Gal. 4:25-26)

3. No more special holy spaces (Matt. 27:51; Heb. 8:2, 9:1, 8, 24-5)

4. No Aaronic high priest (Heb. 4:14–5:10; 7:27-8)

5. No Levitical priests (1 Pet. 2:5; Heb. 7:23

6. No animal sacrifices (Heb. 9:9-10)

7. No Sabbaths or feast days (Col. 2:16-17)

8. No clean and unclean distinctions (Col. 2:21)

9. No food laws (Col. 2:21; 1 Tim. 4:3)

10. No obligation to keep the whole Torah (Gal. 3:15-18; 5:3)

11. No circumcision (Gal 5:6, 6:15; 1 Cor. 7:19)

12. No Mosaic covenant (Gal. 4:21-31; Heb. 8:6, 7, 13, 22; 12:24)

13. No chosen nation (Col. 3:12; 1 Pet. 2:9)

14. No religiously significant genealogies (Matt. 1:1-17; Luke 3:23-38; 1 Tim. 1:4; Titus 3:9)

15. No Jew/Gentile division of humanity (Acts 10 & 11; Eph. 2:11-22; 2 Pet. 2:9)

The final two points—the main subject of this little book—are perfectly consistent with and logically follow from the first thirteen sweeping changes. With the coming of the Messiah, the people of Israel fulfilled their vocation, the purposes for which God chose them. Their history reached its goal when Jesus was born, suffered, died, rose again, and ascended into heaven to inaugurate his new kingdom. And after his gracious offer of forgiveness between Pentecost and the destruction of the Temple, their divinely sanctioned existence as God's chose people came to an end. If everything that defined them is now gone, and all the services they rendered have been completed and are now obsolete, what would be the point of their continued existence as God's favored, chosen people? Especially when they continue to do today that which caused their downfall in the first century—reject God's grace offered to them in Christ.

Does forever mean forever? Yes. The faithful Israelite Messiah Jesus and those united to him, his body, the Church, are the recipients of all the promises made to the faithful people of God in Scripture. He lives and reigns forever and so shall we. "So let no one boast in men. For all things are yours, whether Paul or Apollos or Cephas or the world or life or death or the present or the future—all are yours, and you are Christ's, and Christ is God's" (1 Cor. 21b-23).

Parting Clarifications

I need to make a few clarifying remarks, for in today's milieu it is almost guaranteed that someone will draw the wrong conclusions from what I have written. Nothing I have written here justifies hatred for contemporary Jews. Modern Jews have no claim on the pre-Christ promises, and they are not God's chosen people, but that doesn't mean they are forever cursed. The first-century Jews and Jerusalem were given the opportunity to repent of their rejection of the Messiah (Acts 1-28). Many did. At the end of that transitional period "all Israel" was saved (Rom. 11:26). But others, especially many apostate leaders in Jerusalem, hardened themselves and were judged by Jesus, as he prophesied (Matt. 24, Mark 13, Luke 21; 1 Thess 2:14-16; Rev. 1-22).

That was almost two thousand years ago. Today's modern Jews are like any other ethnic or religious group: they are simply one of the many peoples and nations that are called to repentance and faith in the risen and reigning Jesus. Modern Jews have the same responsibilities toward God and need salvation through Christ just like any other contemporary ethnic and cultural community.

Further, the nation-state of Israel today should be judged like any other nation, with the same standards to which we hold other nations accountable. Unfortunately, America has not always been clear about the rationale for our support of Israel. If the United States finds the nation of Israel to be a trustworthy ally in the Middle East, it should be because they share our values and support our interests in the Middle East, not because we fear being cursed by God for not blessing the sons of Abraham. This is not the place to argue for or against political support for the modern state of Israel. What I have tried to do is expose the erroneous biblical-theological arguments made by many American Christians for unconditional support for modern Jews and the Jewish state based on their supposed favored status as God's chosen people.

Further Reading

Jordan, James B. *Through New Eyes: Developing a Biblical View of the World.* Eugene, OR: Wipf & Stock, 1999.

Leithart, Peter. *Delivered from the Elements: Atonement, Justification, Mission.* Downers Grove, IL: Intervarsity Press, 2016.

__________. *Revelation 1-11.* London: Bloomsbury T&T Clark, 2018.

Staples, Jason A. *Paul and the Resurrection of Israel: Jews, Former Gentiles, Israelites.* Cambridge, UK: Cambridge University Press, 2024.